HALF MYSTIC PRESS

is an international, independent publishing house dedicated to the celebration of music in all of its forms. HMP publishes three to five books of prose, poetry, and experimental work per year, as well as two issues per year of *Half Mystic Journal.* For more information, books similar to this one, and submission guidelines, please visit www.halfmystic.com.

praise for
crowd surfing with god

"*Crowd Surfing With God* is a book of consistent breaking and re-fixing. I love most how the book pulls at the edges of all of Adrienne Novy's many parts, stepping outside the binaries of love, loss, identity, genre, and all manner of things holy. There is sharp language, and palpable imagery, yes. But what works best about the book is how it grabs a reader by each arm, dragging them into many new directions, where something new and impossibly bright is waiting to be discovered."

> —*Hanif Abdurraqib,* author of *The Crown Ain't Worth Much* and *They Can't Kill Us Until They Kill Us*

"All of us cry and yet still the next day arrives, whether we like it or not, but it presents itself with an invitation to move forward in life. Strength lives within vulnerability. This book is a prime example of just that. It's inspiring to anyone who has felt like a bit of a misfit, a black sheep, or a burden. It's a gift to be able to share our stories and rise above, so I hope that it is well received and keeps on inspiring others to live through our pain. Those who get to read this can find relation and comfort in the most sincere manner and are lucky to have stumbled upon such an eye opening book. Thank you, Adrienne."

"Throughout this book, Adrienne asks the reader to not only reveal their softness, but revel in it. This book is a dance party, a late night confession, and a victory anthem to belt in the car. It invites us to praise the music that saved us and the people we sing along with. Holy is our survival. Fierce is our living. Let us celebrate what created us by not destroying us, and sing the chorus one more time."

FIRST PRINTING, APRIL 2018
HALF MYSTIC PRESS
www.halfmystic.com

EDITED *by* DANIE SHOKOOHI
and TOPAZ WINTERS

DESIGNED *by* REBEKAH MARKILLIE
and TOPAZ WINTERS

ISBN-13: 978-1-948552-02-8
ISBN-10: 1-948552-02-7

CROWD SURFING WITH GOD

Adrienne Novy

A
Half Mystic Press
Publication

for sick kids
for queer people of faith
for punks

a blessing over the stratocaster

blessed are you, lord our god, tour manager
of the universe, for gifting us the backbone of song,
for calling it a bridge—

set list

in bloom

my body sings like a vase full of bellflowers. i am a woodwind musician teaching myself to play guitar. there are petals on the tenon rings. blossoms splitting the fretboard. phrygian dominant prayer. o, how my softness bites so clean. bottom lip scar tissue. neck deep in power chords.

patti smith taught me of calluses, clipped fingernails, the seven ways of going, the blessing of the vulnerable.

there are coral beads in my thyroid. a budding callus on my thumb. rustle of spring. my clarinet is an extension of me. the crocus of my voice. the bent prayer of my tongue. i heard a song & then dug it out of my throat.

catch & release

as the nurse draws blood, my veins roll & collapse. she angles carefully for a squirm of blue, calls it fishing. she re-ties the tourniquet, & my body becomes a catfish not fooled by lures, fighting with the hook tugging at skin.

minnesota called it a winter emergency; we called it revival

if you blow the oak off its hinges, panel the space with the kind of glass only you can see out of. saint paul screaming with ice. séance of the moose blood. full-bellied roar. look, kid, i get it: you're sad & that bites. i listen to a lot of pop punk & each band starts to sound the same. but then again, so does my grief. or the way i grieve it. my head is full of tiny moving parts. my throat is cold. i think it's gonna snow tonight.

crowd surfing with god

the Patron Saint of Warped Tour invented stage
diving, the Universe granted us with song,
God taught the sky how to jump, built a bowling
alley in the clouds to give us thunderstorms,

& all of the dead dogs I have ever loved are
howling, barking out the lightning,
Heaven's Gates are constructed out of four basic
chords, a capo on the fret of thunderstorms,

whenever the water overflowed, it gurgled out
piano-drums from the maws of fish,
the mud at the cartridge of the river crusted into
vinyl, ethylene thunderstorms,

the cracking is from a throne of Pernambuco
wood breaking in a sixteenth note of a 6/8 bar,
low rumbling from the clouds is called brontide,
timpani tuning, percussion lessons, thunderstorms,

rain left small blessings on stained glass windows
of Philadelphia churches, composed
eulogies, melody dense as cumulus.
meteorologists predicted thunderstorms,

The Creation of Music : The Creation of Grief ::
Octave Identification : Storm Chasing,
a tour called *NO CLOSER TO HEAVEN*; snares,
eardrums, erupted into thunderstorms,

our angry stages of grief became rivers draining
between two backyards,

the pastor's words came pouring down like rain.

cat's in the cradle

if you are diagnosed with Cat Eye Syndrome as an infant, you will struggle to keep food down, gagging on the spoon in your mother's hand, your body mired in the silver melody of a hospital.

when you are sick, your father will teach you the lyrics of Harry Chapin songs.

> *my child arrived just the other day... came to the world in the usual way...*

then, years of trips to the ER, wrapping into the pulse of an IV.

the doctors have discovered your intestines strangling a coiled mess around your stomach.

your insides wringing themselves out.

lights

i know the fluorescent lights of an emergency room better than a synagogue or a church.

if heaven is real, i pray it doesn't smell like iodoform.

i hunch over a pink plastic bedpan, my body regurgitating her gospel.

ode to caitin stickels

girl's got fangs / a bold statement lip / cat eye
keratin sharp / crescent retinas / goddess of the ring
light / don't you dare declaw this bitch / these scars call
for a celebration / more beauty mark than burden /
Caitin, you taught me to look at my malformed shoulder
& decorate it in tulle / tattoos / say, *fuck you*
to the photoshop / let the jewel of bone beg the
camera to focus / low muscle tone model material /
with fused teeth / yowling at purple mountain's dusk /
sphynx girl as super blood moon! / my body! /
my body! / willing to love the light!

shark bait

i am seven years old & playing in the sandbox
at the park district pool, telling Avie
i am extra careful because one of my arms does not go up
all the way:

that's as far as it goes because the bones overlap.
i wish it wasn't a bad shoulder or easy deep end prey.
the ball & socket are like aquarium gravel in a tank cleaner.

she does not believe me & forces my left arm
straight above my head.

we are the bright side!!!

every teen with a guitar is quick to become a god. or an angel. depends on who breaks their snare-drum head during a concert first. band practice in Joe's mom's garage?—that's church. these sharpie'd converse?—our Sunday best. the lead vocalist?—our Lord & Savior.

bless summers of black baseball tees, the ways they stuck to us like Catholic guilt.

bless learning to skateboard, RJ tuning the Holy Ghost of their bass & the way the cornfields in our patch of suburbia tilt their ears towards a genesis.

the band name came to RJ in a dream,
it's a tradition, naming a musical group this way: RJ's father named his band from an unconscious calling. he & his friends still resurrect a stage every friday night.

i listen to Joe & RJ rehearse & breathe during the rests. when they come home from college, i bring my clarinet into Joe's basement & i learn songs by hearing a note & then playing it.

i have a really good feeling about this, RJ says, about the band, & we all do too, *this will make a hell of a story one day.*

we heal & agree to meet up again tomorrow.
the imaginary audience in the driveway hums,
we break into our loudest prayer.

*diary entry from the ronald
mcdonald house near loyola
children's hospital, july 26th,
2004, summer after second
grade, age 8*

dear diary,

when me & my family went to a *[hotel]*
[house] home for sick children & their families,
we found the *[secret room]*
[magical treasure cave full of giant teddy bears & dolls]
[place you want to hide when the anesthesia wears off]
tender cathedral of soft.

gerard way talks me down from a panic attack

they're these terrors and it's like // **anxiety is an insomniac full of angry noise //** *it feels like as if somebody was gripping my throat// and squeezing //* **makes me want to tear out my own hair like restringing a guitar //** *they're these terrors, and it's like //* **an empty ghost follicle brain coated in vinyl //** *it feels like as if somebody was gripping my //* **paramour mansion skull //** *they're these terrors and it's like //* *it feels like as if somebody was gripping my throat //* *and squeezing //* *they're these terrors, and it's like //* **music is a preventative for self-destruction //** *it feels like as if somebody was gripping my //* *they're these terrors and it's like //* **put on your headphones — i'd much rather smash a guitar than watch you crack yourself in half //** *it feels like as if somebody was gripping my throat //* *and squeezing //* *they're these terrors, and it's like //* **you just gotta focus on the music & your breathing //** *it feels like as if somebody was gripping my //* *they're these terrors and it's like //* *it feels like as if somebody was gripping my throat //* *and squeezing //* **anxiety cuts off your air, but kid, your lungs — they too are an instrument //** *it feels like as if somebody was gripping my throat //* *and squeezing //* *they're these terrors, and it's like //* **you have to inhale for four counts //**

it feels like as if somebody was gripping my // they're these
terrors and it's like *//* it feels like as if somebody was gripping
my throat *//* **hold for seven** *// and squeezing //* **let it out for**
eight *// they're these*

terrors, and it's like // it feels like as if somebody was gripping
my throat // and squeezing // they're these terrors, and it's
like // it feels like as if somebody was gripping my // they're
these terrors and it's like // **you're safe—you're safe you're**
safe i promise *// it feels like as if somebody was gripping my*
throat // they're these terrors, and it's like // it feels like as if
somebody was gripping my // they're these terrors and it's
like // it feels like as if somebody was gripping my throat // and
squeezing // **you will fall into a dreamless sleep** *// they're*
these terrors, and it's like // **ritardando of the**
benzodiazepine *// it feels like as if somebody was gripping my*
// they're these terrors and it's like // **tomorrow will be fresh**
& blank staff paper *// it feels like as if somebody was*
gripping my throat // and squeezing // they're these terrors, and
it's like // it feels like as if somebody was gripping my // they're
these terrors and it's like // it feels like as if somebody was
gripping my throat // and squeezing // **healing will open on a**
new chord

// it feels like as if somebody was gripping my // **simple &**
dissonant—the purest kind of honest

my clarinet speaks

i taught you how to pray in your own language,
to growl in the back of your throat,
the embouchure of a sob as it spoons & dips out
midnight.

you did not have a Bat Mitzvah,
so you grew up with a band at your back,
tech rehearsal shiva. we can't inherit everything:
your mother's upbringing in New York, the Buffalo
Shuffle. your understanding of God is sight reading,
faith held in key change, muscle memory.
you were taught to cry by the full-bodiness of
the shelter in your mouth, jaw dropping out underneath,
lungs swallowing a night full of stars.

i am facing you East to pray.
i am pointing the music in your spirit towards home.

billie joe armstrong & i come out to each other

in the name of talk therapy, punk rock, & the state of California, let's get really queer on the chorus. Jesus can kick it with us when suburbia gets uncomfortable. i'd rather go to hell than never write an honest song again.

whether or not you've been aware of your own bisexuality, God still calls us her favorite band. i don't think a deity had everything figured out when she created the universe. Mom & Dad will never understand how big our love can be, but that doesn't mean you will never meet someone who gets it.

i've got the words *seventeen & confused* tattooed onto my first fender, so i understand exactly why you're scared. it's okay if you don't feel ready to label things yet.

we've still got our friends & we still have the radio.
i promise you're gonna be fine.

pretty in my brand new scars

[Verse 1]

Oh, secondhand   emergency

Say your prayers   [to the sutures]

        [hospital chapel]

[Verse 2]

        [you]   in brand new scars

hate   [a lot]   about yourself [& the ways you blister]

        [ugly hallelujah, skin tape sinner]

[Chorus]

[you] say your prayers   &

[call the surgery an orchestra of steel]

[clean off the guitar frets with a scalpel]

        [repeat the baptism of the intravenous therapy]

say your prayers

[say your prayers]   *say your prayers*

if the honeybees die, then we will die with them

Carrie Fisher died within a milky-clouded sky sleep & I imagine her mother's ventricles clogging with honey.

If heaven is a hive, I want to swim in it, like the way a Falcon does with space, cosmos beading off its wings.

Loss is an act of inheritance: two houses entombed in amber, carbonite; family photographs, antiques webbed in hexagons.

My body is a white dress sewn of ash, Prozac urn, wishful wedding-funeral. Inside of me lives my father's mother & my mother's mother & everything my mother taught me, too. I call Carrie my Space Mom to make myself feel closer to the newest star of grave soil.

After we are long long dead & this planet's two suns have been extinguished, we will burst with light to greet the world again as keepers of a millennia, the royalty of galaxies & garden trellises: a fresh & new & brilliant hope.

my retinas as a solar eclipse

trisomy of Chromosome 22—
                        a fragmented holy. coloboma halo,

fractal iris,
                        felinus pupils;

                the midnight
                                        slink underneath Jacob's ladder.

genetics doctor as a god.

elliot alderson processes grief for the first time

o, father. o, holy virgin motherboard. o, great spear-phisher trojan horse honey pot garden of eden. *please tell me you're seeing this, too:* the naive who swallow the corrupted & call it eucharist. the white gauze as it turns my blood a holy color. *i pray to you to regain control.* let me rest. let my voice cut through hymnal static. let me rest. let me say amen. amen. amen. amen. amen. 4m3n.

let's make this a game

distract yourself from the histamine welts.

       ask your mother to read *Junie B. Jones* to you
       & the girl who just got her tonsils out.

start a round of Simon Says—
epidural scratch—
(Simon did not say scratch.)

       scar hides   go seek.

Pediatric Trivia: dial on the hospital room phone,
be the first to correctly answer the riddle &

       win a prize from the red toy wagon.

if you walk with your IV all the way down the hall, mom
will let you go pick out a new book.

you, the Sick Kid, were *so brave* today,
swallowed the hospital library whole,
called it taking your medicine.

diary of a young girl

if you lifted the roof off of my childhood bedroom, the flashlight hours spent curled under blankets, reading past bedtime, could brighten a house of prayer.

when i was nine, i checked out *Anne Frank: The Diary of a Young Girl* from the local library.

i asked my Jewish mother & Roman Catholic father which faith i was supposed to practice. i did not have a Bat Mitzvah or a Confirmation, but Anne & i were both door slams of curious girls. this was how i looked for something to believe in.

i was not old enough to fully understand the diary, or to fully understand myself, but searching for god in a library is gospel to a child.

in fourth grade, a girl in my class told me her great-great-uncle was a nazi, said he would have killed my whole family. i left Anne Frank at home.

when i was sixteen, i had a crush on a boy from my town's Jewish center, but also thought about kissing my friend Gracie. i bet she tasted like sparkling grape juice, the champagne of a star, the words from the best book i had ever read.

on my thirteenth birthday, during Hanukkah, my mother gave me my Star of David, a multifacet of gold. on her thirteenth birthday, Anne Frank unwrapped her diary, not knowing the whole world was a teenager yearning for a best friend.

before Anne Frank's diary was published, her father redacted entries where she questioned her sexuality, lifted away arguments with her mother from the final transcript, claimed he did this out of respect for the dead.

when you are Jewish & queer, you die on every page of every book. you convince yourself that the sky is the only place you are allowed to live. i think about how quickly i would have unwritten myself if my father had found all of my truths.

Anne wrote about how she saw this universe: the fights in the annex, her desires & masturbation, about liking both boys & girls.

if the unedited version of the diary did not exist, i would have continued to tear chapters out of my body, ban the library of me, burn the candlelight down in my mouth until I am both unlit match & choked sky, burning from the inside out.

the pop punk bible

in the beginning, god was a fifteen-year-old girl & in the beginning, the earth was without form & void & so god created MySpace & god wore sleeveless denim jackets & shopped at Hot Topic & thought about stretching her ears & in the beginning god said, *let there be alternative rock music in the early 2000s* & so god plucked a comic book artist from New Jersey & handed him notebooks & microphones & electric guitars, begging for a ballad & god told him to create until he felt himself breaking

& My Chemical Romance created so much loud, their name became shattered glass & Gerard Way accepted all the outcasts & every venue's barstool splintered into pews & god smashed years worth of beer bottles & pills & this stained glass resurrection formed Fall Out Boy & Panic! At the Disco & eve did not come from adam, but they both cracked their ribs in the mosh pit & threw leather jackets to the wolves

& My Chemical Romance still broke & god wanted to fix the brokenness but then realized the healthiness of being apart, how no breathing space between artistry & healing almost killed the band that saved her life & god bought all the albums & god still knows all the words & god listened to them over & over & over again until her parents pounded on her bedroom door & made her turn her music down

& when god wanted to kill herself, when thoughts of suicide became a kickdrum inside her skull, My Chemical Romance grabbed her by the collar of her tour t-shirt & screamed, *THERE IS NOTHING WORTH HURTING YOURSELF OVER. NOTHING IS WORTH TAKING YOUR LIFE OVER. DO YOU UNDERSTAND?* & god broke down like an old set of speakers & My Chemical Romance held her until she fell asleep & no longer wanted to be buried in a guitar case

& this was the first blessing to Helena that faded out like a song & the prayers ended with *so long & goodnight* & god stayed alive for another night & then another night & then another night & that meant the night was good & the terrors stopped & the plugs sparked & stadiums crackled with light & life carried on & it was good & it was good & it was so fucking good.

warped tour as the temple that took 22 years to build, tinley park, july 19th, 2014

passing a water bottle back & forth, my friends resurface from a Motionless in White set:

thank god you weren't there. you would have been terrified.

yeah, the moment sound popped through the amps, the crowd surged into a wave of sweat, the seafoam of cheap beer.

it was like being inside of The Ocean that swallowed The Whale that swallowed Jonah, but damn, was it worth fighting the current. this left-over adrenaline is such a fucking miracle, i swear that Heaven must've kissed me.

i wish i had a river

Joni Mitchell's voice crosses over the break & when the ice gives, I will treat the cold as the hurt that I deserve. My bed, a glacier. A flock of toe picks.

Healing is a cold breath of blue migration,
bison digging for sweetgrass beneath the frost.

My friend changes the radio station in his car as geese soar above the overpass. The drums align with the beating of their wings. He tells me not to talk to him anymore. I ask my roommates to take me out skating.

There should be more reasons than a thaw & a good song for me to want to leave the house. The weight of my bones moves slow. I have yet to forgive the ache I once created.

I should be south of here already.

last breakfast

today is the day i finally get to go home. my tummy scars ache & the bandages pinch. the doctors took out my appendix along with unknotting the shoelaces of my stomach & intestines. my body is now a game of Two Truths & a Lie.

mom serves chocolate chip yogurt as a celebration breakfast. my brother & i bring our bowls into the Ronald McDonald House family room to watch The Brave Little Toaster on the small TV. Blankie is paused drifting mid-air as i rush to the bathroom & my stomach releases weeks worth of healing into the toilet. mom gently rubs my upper back & hushes me as i am bent over, crying. the drive back to the hospital is quiet.

my chemical romance headlines the reading festival with brian may, england, august 26th, 2011

the first anthemic riff of *Welcome to the Black Parade* begins

    & Ray Toro & Brian May bend back like they have wings tearing out of their black shirts & Ray gives Gerard the most joyous smile, as though this is their newest happiness & G instructs the crowd to put their fists in the air, which is concert-speak for, *there's so much light brimming from the stage & i want you to catch it & let it fill up every lonely night of craving, every night of the heavy cold wanting you to die & i want you to remember how rock opera carried you on to put one foot in front of the other to take a fucking shower!* & so i make a mental list of all the ways to be better & how this concert arena is full of recovery &

Frank is screaming his head off on backup vocals like the angel of death is searing right through him & the scorpion on his neck stings a chorus like all of this was worth it & Mikey doesn't talk a whole lot, but his bones are saying everything honest & exhausting that he's wanted to say over the past ten years & the crowd is dancing to a tomorrow to survive in & strobe lights are exploding on two & four &

Gerard, the purest beacon of red for miles, asks the crowd,

ARE YOU READY TO OPEN UP A BIG GIANT BLACK FUCKING HOLE & DANCE WITHIN IT? & that catapults thousands of bodies into the first verse to a heaven we never really believed in but on bad days we wished we did & goddamn if we aren't grateful that we didn't see it sooner & Gerard is thankful for this & for the electricity of living & he no longer owns this powerhouse & hasn't since 2006 & accepts all that is meant to be & he points the microphone to the audience singing along to every word like it is the reclaiming of their healing & a portal into a shining universe roars above us & i never saw My Chemical Romance live before they broke up, but i imagine this is how forgiveness sounds: the tunnel of noise & confetti bursting for one of its last times, a message the band has been waiting on for what feels like centuries. a signifying. the passing on of a torch.

rhapsody in blue

i stare at the ceiling as the nurses monitor my heart; its slow slow & its quick quick. my valves backwash cerulean; blood slips through like a leaky key, loves to swing dance, snare syncopation, skips like brush percussion.

in high school, the music department took a trip to Walt Disney World. we played a Porgy & Bess medley in the park. i don't remember what happened but my heart did its dance & my friends pushed me around in a wheelchair in the Animal Kingdom.

i am now 22 & recently bought a jazz mouthpiece & my sound is as open as a vein. pops out all celestial & the RN wants to prick it. if i am healthier now than i ever have been, can i sing the Sick Kid Jazz Standard of *"This Could Be Worse"*? squeak into it again like old tap shoes? shuffle & ball-change into a hospital gown?

the gliding a clarinetist does in George Gershwin classics is through mouth control & muscle memory. lifting gentle fingers. deep lung work & oxygen exchange. my body knows how to play a lot of songs, this chromatic prolapse, forgetting to purse the edges of its valves to prevent color from seeping through.

lupus

verb

1. to be the stubborn dog refusing to heel
2. to create constellations out of blood cells
3. to swallow the moon
4. to cough up the telescope

> synonyms: *butterfly rash. increased risk of miscarriage. joint/muscle aches. extreme fatigue. flu-like symptoms. night sweats. inflammation of the tissues covering internal organs with associated chest &/or abdominal pain. seizures. cerebral problems. headaches, migraines. oral/nasal ulcers. kidney problems. anaemia. swollen glands. poor blood circulation causing the tips of fingers & toes to turn white then blue on exposure to cold. blood tremolo. hypothermic lullaby.*

> antonyms: *coumadin. vitamin d. warfarin. plaquenil. rheumatologist. gastrologist. ear, nose & throat physician. dermatologist. cardiologist. the syringe removing scarlet from the irises. ingesting a flower nursery full of pills every morning.*

there is at present no cure for lupus but careful monitoring of the disease & a treatment programme with medication adjusted as appropriate enables the condition to be controlled.

most patients being able to live a normal life span. doctors will usually only keep the patient on high impact medication for as short a period as possible.

> can you repeat the tests again, please? what is its genetic root? blood clot of origin: the unnamed star from which it came? the diagnostic pronunciation, galactic etymology of chronic illness? how many different ways can my mother's pain be used in a sentence?

i lit you a candle in every cathedral across europe (even though i've never left the states)

Patron Saint of

>basketball trophies,
>church singers & pillow fort kings,
>icicle light christening,
>dead loved ones passing on as lyrics.

/

I've seen my mother break down like this before. we got the call that you died in your sleep, so she tore open a pillow. a blizzard ripped through the Midwest.

/

O, Dear Saint of Cassette Tapes, Creator of Clean Snow & Songs to Cry to Sleep to, I know you're headlining Heaven's Bandshell & playing lead guitar. my family does not pray to the rapture of pop punk that I do, but that

doesn't mean they don't believe in something. everyone
I've ever cherished keeps returning as a holiday.

my new medication is purple
& fall out boy is too

My therapist reminds me that my thoughts are just thoughts: the repertoire of my head, cognitive distortions as a shitty mixtape. *It's just a storm,* she says, *a wave of bad noise that will eventually pass.*

I cannot find a pill cutter, so my dad halves a week's worth of medication for me with a steak knife—splicing a whole note, the anatomy of a measure.

I listen to songs by sad men. I drink two cups of coffee & am still exhausted. From the time I fell apart to when I moved home for treatment, Patrick Stump has belted out 21 new songs.

My illnesses scream that I don't deserve to create art, let alone experience it at all. The noise so loud that cells of violet bleed into my field of vision. Magical thinking mercy burner. I blast my favorite songs to brave the riptide. I practice my DBT skills. I pay attention to the overtones.

I feel my pulse in order to be present. I tell myself that when I get better, I'll go to more concerts that are louder than my own brain. I will cry this neon joy until it washes out the sun.

I am learning to not let my intrusive thoughts get through the venue door. My Wise Mind buys all the tickets, invites memories of the people who love me. I dance so the room is full.

on building a shrine

a sanitized cardinal feather.

the ribcage of a hummingbird.

recordings of a goldfinch call.

six *bonne maman* jam jars, washed, reused for drinking seltzer & orange juice.

a small tin box with a robin egg lid.

snowflakes on black paper. a plastic magnifying glass.

a yellow, faded post-it note. a trembling wrist. *Grandma Dayis loves you.*

family recipe for oatmeal waffles—only to be made on Father's Day, Christmas morning, & Other Special Occasions.

a wine cylinder containing a can of cherry filling. an IOU for Grandma Sheila's famous cherry cake.

nineteen monarch butterfly wings.

a journal of pressed flowers: carnations, daffodils, wildflowers from a prairie somewhere in Illinois.

a photo of Freeway, the stubborn dachshund-poodle mix with curly black fur & a graying beard, melted underneath the dinner table, whining.

all that grows here

it started with my female classmates blossoming into
women first // then the thorns that wrapped around
my abdomen & dug me back into bed // then
the boy who noticed the patches of hair // how
he called me a rodent // then the man who asked how
anyone would want to kiss me if i looked like this // then
the tweezing // the stinging of hot wax // the laser hair
removal appointments // the dermatologist as a careful
gardener // the birth control // the pesticide of
sleep // the panic attacks // then the apologies of
when white hotel sheets flooded into a poppy field //
then the sleeping on top of towels & the
embarrassment of men & then the pools of
blood because there is always blood //

when the tests came back & the diagnosis was confirmed,
my mother called me while she was gardening //
my mother loves gardening the way that i love
poetry // we both want everything to be perfect //
my mother: the artist whose blood is my blood //
earthen caregiver // Jewish inheritor of the clotting
of worry // whose first child was a miscarriage //

who would check to see if the family who lived in our old house still tended to the flowers //
this is how I taught myself to call my body a weed: dormant girl // late bloomer // awkward form of unlovable // sprouting in ways I shouldn't //

when my mother explains that Polycystic Ovarian Syndrome means I might not be able to have children // I ask myself how anyone will love this garden if nothing can ever grow here //
but this body deserves forgiveness // after all the breaking // after shame became the hardest storm // the coldest month // tulip bulbs in frozen soil //
I am re-learning what it means to fully love myself //
that winter is still a gorgeous season // even when all the life // is hiding

notes

"In Bloom" is titled after Neck Deep's song under the same name, from their album, *The Peace and The Panic*. The poem is after Anis Mojgani, Bill Moran, and Sabrina Benaim.

"Minnesota Called it a Winter Emergency; We Called it Revival" is based after "Common Cold" by Tiny Moving Parts from their album *Celebration*. It was inspired by Ollie Schminkey and references the band Moose Blood.

"Crowd Surfing With God" is a broken ghazal after Aaron Samuels. The last line is a lyric from "Cigarettes & Saints" by The Wonder Years. The poem also references The Wonder Years' songs "You in January" and "I Wanted So Badly to Be Brave". It was heavily influenced by "Hallelujah" by Leonard Cohen and the work of Hanif Abdurraqib.

"Cat's in the Cradle" is after Harry Chapin's song of the same name, and borrows a line from the song.

"Shark Bait" was heavily influenced by the film *Finding Nemo*.

"We Are the Bright Side!!!" is after Danez Smith and

Hanif Abdurraqib. The poem is for Joe Soldati and RJ Ramanauskas.

"Gerard Way Talks Me Down From a Panic Attack" uses a quote from a recording of Gerard Way talking about the night terrors he experienced while the band My Chemical Romance stayed in the Paramour Mansion. The title of the poem and the quote are both from MCR's song "Sleep", from their album *The Black Parade*. The poem is after Bill Moran's *Charcoal Healing Ritual* poems from his collection "Oh God Get Out Get Out", Patrick Kindig's "Prayer of Supplication", and the work of George Abraham.

"My Clarinet Speaks" is after Sterling Higa and the Yiddish song "Di Nakht", performed by The Klezmatics and written by Hirsh Glick. Translated, the song's full title means, "Quiet, the Night is Full of Stars".

"Billie Joe Armstrong & I Come Out to Each Other" was influenced by Billie Joe's interview in a 1995 issue of *The Advocate*. It is written after "Coming Clean", from Green Day's album *Dookie*.

Pretty In My Brand New Scars is a partial erasure poem of "Hallelujah" by Panic! at the Disco from their album *Death of a Bachelor*.

The quote "please tell me you're seeing this too" in "Elliot Alderson Processes Grief for the First Time" is from Season 1 of the television show *Mr. Robot*, written and created by Sam Esmail.

"The Pop Punk Bible" references the songs "Helena (So Long and Goodnight)", "Honey, This Mirror Isn't Big Enough for the Two of Us", "Thank You for the Venom", and a video recording of Gerard Way giving a speech on mental health at one of the shows on My Chemical Romance's *The Black Parade* tour.

"Warped Tour as the Temple That Took 22 Years to Build, Tinley Park, July 19th 2014" is after Hanif Abdurraqib and Bill Moran.

"I Wish I Had a River" is after "River" by Joni Mitchell. The last line of this poem is a line borrowed from "A Song for Ernest Hemingway" by The Wonder Years off their album *Burst & Decay*.

"My Chemical Romance Headlines the Reading Festival with Brian May, August 26th, 2011" is after Hanif Abdurraqib and Kaveh Akbar, and uses a quote from Gerard Way spoken in between songs during a concert in London, May 2008.

"Rhapsody in Blue" is after Sabrina Benaim.

"Lupus" is after a prompt by Kevin Kantor. The synonyms in the poem are symptoms of Lupus Antibody Syndrome, found on www.lupusuk.org.uk.

"I Lit You a Candle in Every Cathedral Across Europe (Even Though I've Never Left the States)" is after the song "Cigarettes & Saints" by The Wonder Years. Lyrics from this song are used in the poem's title. It is for Joel.

"My New Medication is Purple & Fall Out Boy is Too" is after "The Last of the Real Ones" and "Sunshine Riptide" from Fall Out Boy's album *M A N I A*.

"On Building a Shrine" is written after a prompt by Sun Yung Shin, which was based on *i, afterlife* by Kristin Prevallet.

"All That Grows Here", "Diary of a Young Girl", and "My Retinas as a Solar Eclipse" were inspired by and brought to fruition because of the work, help, and support of Corva León.

Thank you to Jasper, Brendan, and Max for the English-to-Hebrew translation of "A Blessing Over the Stratocaster".

this mixtape is for sinners

"Say Amen (Saturday Night)"
     by *Panic! At the Disco*

"No Closer to Heaven"
     by *The Wonder Years*

"Seven Ways of Going"
     by *Patti Smith*

"In Bloom"
     by *Neck Deep*

"Favorite"
     by *Tigers Jaw*

"Veins! Veins!! Veins!!!"
     by *Frank Iero and the Patience*

"Common Cold"
     by *Tiny Moving Parts*

"Pastel"
     by *Moose Blood*

"I Wanted So Badly to Be Brave"
     by *The Wonder Years*

"Hallelujah"
>   by *Leonard Cohen,* performed by *Jeff Buckley*

"House of Wolves"
>   by *My Chemical Romance*

"Cats in the Cradle"
>   by *Harry Chapin*

"Church"
>   by *Fall Out Boy*

"A Portrait Of"
>   by *Sorority Noise*

"Jesus of Suburbia"
>   by *Green Day*

"Rock 'N Roll"
>   by *Avril Lavigne*

"Dammit"
>   by *blink-182*

"Sleep"
>   by *My Chemical Romance*

"Shtil Di Nakht is Oygesternt"
>   by *Quadro Nuevo*

"Coming Clean"

by *Green Day*

"Hallelujah"
by *Panic! At the Disco*

"A Song For Ernest Hemingway"
by *The Wonder Years*

"Daughter"
by *Doll Skin*

"Helena (So Long & Good Night)"
by *My Chemical Romance*

"Tring Quarry"
by *Trash Boat*

"River"
by *Joni Mitchell*

"I'm A Mess"
by *Frank Iero and the Patience*

"Welcome to the Black Parade"
by *My Chemical Romance*

"Cigarettes & Saints"
by *The Wonder Years*

"Sunshine Riptide"
by *Fall Out Boy*

"Conversations (Lovely Things Suite Live)"

by *Watsky*

"The Ocean Grew Hands to Hold Me"
by *The Wonder Years*

the books that inspired this one's composition

The Crown Ain't Worth Much
    by *Hanif Abdurraqib*

They Can't Kill Us Until They Kill Us
    by *Hanif Abdurraqib*

Calling a Wolf a Wolf
    by *Kaveh Akbar*

Depression & Other Magic Tricks
    by *Sabrina Benaim*

Autopsy
    by *Donte Collins*

The January Children
    by *Safia Elhillo*

The Diary of a Young Girl
    by *Anne Frank*

The Feather Room
    by *Anis Mojgani*

acknowledgements

Many, many, many thanks and endless love, gratitude, and gentleness to: Hanif Abdurraqib, George Abraham, Kaveh Akbar, Micah Andersen, Ally Ang, Sabrina Benaim, Emma Bleker, Bailey Rose, Kieran Collier, Michelle Chang, Elliot Darrow, Cole Downey, Kayla Farhang, Bernard Ferguson, Cy Ferguson, Siaara Freeman, Dylan García, Rachael Gay, Will Giles, Max Guttman, Guante, Becca Grischow, Kaitlin Hatman, Lyd Havens, Ry Irene, Madeline Happold, Sterling Higa, Adina Kathleen, Jed Lickerman, Eli Mann, Kelsey May, Bill Moran, Joshua Nguyen, Annalee Nock, Namkyu Oh, Brendan Tyler Pell, Shayne Phillips, Bianca Phipps, Jenna Pitstick, Kiley Pohn, Julian Randall, Bryan Renaud, Jess Rizkallah, Michelle Saltouros, EJ Schoenborn, José Soto, Zoey Sparks, Caitin Stickels, Rob Sturma, Meghedi Tamazian, Eric Tu, Meghan Voight, and Laura Young. This project would not have been able to come together without your help, support, kind words, friendship, and creative work. Thank you for the music. Thank you for letting me send you poems.

The Teen Writers and Artists Project for being my first mentors and poetry family, and for reminding me to never forget where I got started. You are the home I will always return to.

My professors at Hamline University: John Colburn, Bill Reichard, Sun Yung Shin, and Katrina Vandenberg, for challenging me, pushing me creatively and academically, supporting me through times of self-doubt, and for helping me grow in ways I never would have imagined.

For Michael Bazan, Janet Greene, and Pat Frederick, my music instructors.

For the Hamline University Poetry Slam teams and Twin Cities poetry community: Jasper, Vi, Kaitlin, Tijqua, Ash, Corva, Blythe, Alix, Taylor, and Jacob. Thank you for holding me, for reminding me to be better.

For the hardworking staff and volunteers of the Ronald McDonald House near the Loyola Children's Hospital. For Dr. Booth, Dr. Oesterle, and Dr. Schulman. For Kelly, Jenny, and the CBT/DBT/ACT skills my therapists have taught me.

And to my mentors: Adam Gottlieb, Corey Dillard, Diana Zwinak, Anne Veague, Sierra DeMulder, Cristopher Gibson, Thressa Johnson, Lewis Mundt, Jen O'Leary Arnett, Brittney Bailey-Cole, Martha Behlow, and Shanny Jean Maney.

This book would not have been possible without the hard work, dedication, belief, and care of Danie Shokoohi, Topaz Winters, Rebekah Markillie, the staff of Half Mystic Press. But most of all, to Daniel Garcia. Thank you for giving me room to sing. You are a good thing.

In loving memory of my grandmothers, Dayis F. Novy and Sheila M. Desbecker.

Thank you to the following literary journals for giving these poems their very first homes, in many different forms:

FreezeRay Poetry, Issue 14: "Elliot Alderson Processes Grief For the First Time", "If the Honeybees Die, Then We Will Die With Them"

Half Mystic Journal, Issue V: Cadenza: "In Bloom"

Maudlin House: "The Pop Punk Bible"

NAILED Magazine: "Diary of a Young Girl", "Last Breakfast", "Let's Make This a Game", "My Retinas as a Solar Eclipse", "Ode to Caitin Stickels"

The Rising Phoenix Review: "Catch & Release", "Cat's in the Cradle", "July 26th, 2004, Summer After Second Grade, Age 8", "Lights", "Shark Bait"

The poems "Catch & Release", "Cat's in the Cradle", "Diary Entry From the Ronald McDonald House Near Loyola Children's Hospital, July 26th, 2004, Summer After Second Grade, Age 8", "Last Breakfast", "Let's Make This a Game", "Lights", "Lucky Fin", "My Retinas as a Solar Eclipse","Ode to Caitin Stickels", and "Shark Bait" can be found in a self-published chapbook, *trisomy 22*.

about the author

Adrienne Novy is a teaching artist, *Bettering American Poetry* nominee, and musician currently living in Saint Paul, MN. Her work can be found in *FreezeRay Poetry, Harpoon Review, Button Poetry, Maudlin House,* and *NAILED Magazine,* with a poem forthcoming in Issue V of *Half Mystic Journal.* She is from the Chicago suburbs and wants to start a band with you.